CONTENTS

THE SEVEN CAPITAL SINS

"For our wrestling is not against flesh and blood; but against principalities and powers, against the rulers of the world of this darkness, against the spirits of wickedness in the high places. Therefore take unto you the armour of God, that you may be able to resist in the evil day, and to stand in all things perfect. Stand therefore, having your loins girt about with truth, and having on the breastplate of justice, and your feet shod with the preparation of the gospel of peace: in all things taking the shield of faith, wherewith you may be able to extinguish all the fiery darts of the most wicked one. And take unto you the helmet of salvation, and the sword of the Spirit (which is the word of God)."

—Ephesians 6:12-17

My Resolution for Today

I resolve this day:

To do all in my power to resist evil and to do good.

To fulfill all the responsibilities of my state in life faithfully.

To observe kindness and honesty in all contacts with my fellowmen.

To preserve complete purity of soul.

If I should be tempted to evil, I will repeat in my heart the words, "Do what is right; Be right; Be cheerful!"

That I may be able to keep this resolution, I ask the help of God, my Creator.

Introduction

The Seven Capital Sins

THERE is a seven-headed monster that each one of us has to fight our whole life through. This monster is SELF-SEEKING or SELF-LOVE. Its seven heads are: **Pride**, **Covetousness**, **Lust**, **Anger**, **Envy**, **Gluttony** and **Sloth**. Bishop Fulton Sheen calls them "the seven pall-bearers of the soul" and gives them the following names: Self-love, inordinate love of money, illicit sex, hate, jealousy, over-indulgence and laziness. (*"Peace of Soul,"* p. 109).

As a result of Original Sin, each one of us has an inborn tendency to assert himself, to make himself the "center" of things, to make his will prevail over that of others. Our great passion is for our highest good, but too often we do not comprehend what this good is, and we seek for it in a wrong way. We need to understand that our highest good is GOD. God has made Himself

1

our last End and Reward. He has shown us the way to Himself through Christ, who called Himself "The Way."

We must recognize our relationship to God as creatures who have the duty to **love and serve Him in the manner He wills and desires**, in order that we may possess Him in Heaven, or "save our souls," as we commonly express it. Now, when we are wrapped up in our own **ego**, even though we may not realize the fact, everything we think, say and do revolves around our own **self**. We are really "seeking self," though we may try to convince ourselves that we are following Christ and seeking God.

Plainly, then, the battle against self-seeking is fought **within our own personality**. Specifically, it is in our **will**. In the fountainhead of self-love and self-will, pride and all the other Capital Sins have their origin and bring forth a host of offspring, great and small. If we are strongly motivated by self-seeking, we will seldom "deny" ourselves, as Our Lord taught, by charity, love, sacrifice, humility, obedience, patience, generosity, or whatever the calls of duty and virtue may be. Instead, our self-love will nourish the vices and we will become more and more ensnared in them.

To pursue the path of self-love is continually to refuse love to God, and such a course is a great danger to salvation. No soul can enter Heaven until it has been purged of all self-love and self-will and exists only for God; that is to say, until it is **sanctified**. Probably for most persons who are saved, a great part of this purging has to be done in Purgatory, because the soul did not do it on earth. But should a soul—or, to be personal—should **we** reject the will of God for our own self-will and self-love even until death, God would be forced to reject us for all eternity, because we had rejected Him. Such a rejection means eternal damnation. Our state would then be unchangeably fixed in self-love and hatred of God, and in Hell we would simply be a "mad center unto ourself"—an ego which must endure without end the unendurable, the unceasing torture of being drawn toward God, and yet being walled-up in its own eternally hate-filled self.

A knowledge of the myriad disguises in which the Seven Capital Sins mask themselves can enable us to come to self-knowledge and help us carry on a successful warfare by practicing the opposite virtues. It is impossible for us to combat an enemy whom we do not know, whom we do not see, or whom, perhaps, we mistake for a friend. Yet often this is actually the case with these vices, especially with pride and sloth.

It is the purpose of this booklet to give some insight into the **nature** of the Capital Sins, at least naming some of the manifold actions which have their root in a particular vice. This knowledge of the **character**, **degrees**, **acts** and **family relationships** of the seven vices will, we hope, be helpful to those who find it hard to examine themselves in their regard, since examinations of conscience often give only the **names** of the Capital Sins.

An early writer, in keeping with the spirit of his time, brings home the viciousness of the Capital Sins by depicting them under the forms of animals. Pride is characterized as a **lion**; covetousness or avarice as a **fox**; lust as a **scorpion**; anger as a **unicorn**, "which beareth on his nose the horn with which he butteth at all whom he reacheth";

envy as a venomous **serpent**; gluttony as "the **swine** of greediness"; and sloth as a **bear**.

The same writer says it is the **devil** who incites in us temptations to sins of malice, such as pride, haughtiness, envy and anger, and to the countless other sins that spring from these roots. Because sins of **malice** are more especially sins of the **mind**, or "spiritual" sins, they are more grievous in their nature.

The **flesh**, he says, naturally inclines us to lust and gluttony, to ease and self-indulgence, which are sins of the **body**, or "carnal" sins, and more shameful and disgraceful in the sight of men.

Finally, the **world** urges us to covet wealth, prosperity, honor and other satisfactions, which are only delusions and lead us to fall in love with shadows.

Our Lord probably referred to the seven vices when He spoke of the unclean spirit that goes out of a man and roams through desert places seeking a resting place, and finding none, returns with "seven other spirits more wicked than himself." (*Matt.* 12:45).

Naturally, the oftener we consent to the temptations aroused by any of the vices, the deeper root the vice takes in us, until at length, **habits of sin** are formed which are very hard to break. So we need at all times to be watchful in combating the lesser sins if we are to be victorious in the greater battles we shall have to wage.

Chapter 1

Pride

PRIDE was the **first sin committed**. It was the sin of Lucifer. It was also the root of the Original Sin committed by Adam and Eve.

Pride is the **greatest** of sins because it is the summit of self-love and is directly opposed to submission to God. It is, therefore, the sin **most hated by God**, and the one He punishes most severely. The punishment of the Angels, of Adam and Eve, of Nabuchodonosor, related in the Book of Daniel (4:27-30), bear witness to this.

Pride is likewise the greatest sin because it is the fountainhead of the self-love in which all other sins take root: "From pride all perdition took its beginning." (*Tob.* 4:14). There is a species of pride in **every** sin, whatever may be the individual nature of the sin itself.

Pride is the **most dangerous** of sins,

because it blinds our understanding, and unless something finally makes us realize the truth, we are liable to go on, day after day, in a spiritual self-delusion, imagining our acts to be good and virtuous when certain habits actually may be vicious. When we are blinded by pride, we do not consider our talents and abilities as God's gifts to us, but attribute our good qualities to ourselves, with the right to use them as we see fit.

Everybody is infected with the virus of pride! But there is a particular **kind** of pride in each individual; at least a particular kind **dominates**, though there may be several of its viruses in the same character. This pride determines our temperament or our type of character, or at least is intimately related to it. Searching into our type of pride is very important for obtaining a true knowledge of ourselves, and for making fruitful efforts to root out sin and vice from our life.

If we are of a **sanguine** temperament, our pride takes the form of **self-centeredness.** We want to be the "hub of the wheel"; we want others to notice us. We are touchy and easily offended. Our pride goads us to seek fame, praise, admiration. We fall into vainglory.

If we have a **choleric** temperament, our pride is manifested in a strong **self-will**. We find it hard to submit to others or to yield to their opinions. We are often overbearing, critical, given to arguing, inflated with a sense of superiority, inconsiderate of the rights of others.

If we are **melancholic,** our pride conceals itself under the garb of **self-pity** and **oversensitiveness**. Resentment, harboring grudges, suspicion, and unexpressed hostility are included in it. Often this pride is not recognized for what it is because it conceals itself as such, so we do not confess it as pride.

If we have a **phlegmatic** character, our pride inclines us to **self-complacency** and vanity. We are likely to be shocked by faults in others, but quite satisfied with our own selves.

Pride of superiority makes us want to control the lives of others, to impose ourselves on them, to "domineer" over them. It makes our will rigid and unbending when others assert authority.

It is a self-will and obstinacy that sets us against the will of God, opposes our neighbor and makes us inflexible in carrying out the dictates of our own self-love. Anger, indignation, arrogance, the spirit of contradiction and haughtiness are some of its offspring. This pride is usually rooted in a strongly opinionated mind which makes us refuse to see the light of reason or the truth evidenced by principles of revealed Faith. This unwillingness actually fosters ignorance. It is the pride which keeps many from entering the Church, or returning to the practice of the Faith when they have fallen away.

Closely connected with this kind of pride—or perhaps we should say another name for it—is the **pride of independence**. This leads us to disobedience and insubordination, to contempt and arrogant contradiction, to refusal of advice and assistance, to resentment of reproof by lawful authority, to blasphemy against God, bitter cursing, oaths and irreverences in word and act.

Delusions in regard to our own defects, self-conceit, attributing to ourselves our good qualities of mind, of person or of fortune—rather than to God, reveal **pride of intellect**. Sins against Faith arise from this pride.

The **pride of ambition** leads us to seek positions or offices of honor and dignity by which we prefer ourselves to others, however worthy they may be. It makes us dream up schemes and projects, and undertake things through presumption, even when we are ignorant of how to go about them. Excessive confidence makes us overestimate our abilities. Immoderate desires, vainglory, the desire for praise, ostentation and the immoderate use of necessities of life in order to be more highly thought of, stem from this pride. It leads to flattery and hypocrisy.

We may have a **pride of spiritual vanity**, imagining ourselves to be perfect and our acts always virtuous or finding a thousand reasons to diminish their gravity or excuse our faults when we do acknowledge them.

Our pride may dress itself in the guise of **naturalism**, in which case we practice no restraint in our behavior, no modesty in our language, no respect in our obedience; we are deceitful in our humility, caustic in our conversation, inveterate in our hatred, a foe to submission, greedy of power, desirous of supplanting others, indolent in action and work. We act through impulse and meddle in the affairs of others. We wish to know everything through unrestrained curiosity. We like to be always talking, even of what we do not understand.

We may have a pride which makes us **cynical**. If so, we speak sarcastically and use cutting words. We ridicule others, scold and misjudge them.

Pharisaical pride leads us to boastfulness and to criticism of others. It makes us overtalkative; it leads to lies and contradictions; to esteeming high birth or social rank above virtue. Haughtiness of manner, disdaining to associate with those we believe to be inferior, arise from it. It manifests itself by a legalism in our actions, causing us to fulfill our duties without spirit, but with hypocrisy.

Our pride may hide itself in **sensitiveness**, or self-pity. In this case we are over-anxious about what others think of us. We brood over imagined wrongs and do not easily forgive others. Closely linked to this form of pride is the **pride of timidity**, which stems from unreasonable fear. It makes us fearful of others' opinions, so that we cater to human respect. Under its impulse we fail to act when we should, because a groundless fear holds us in the bonds of a spiritual sloth that paralyzes our efforts and makes us incapable of determination, and so we let opportunities pass by unused.

The **pride of scrupulosity** fixes our attention on wrong things, so that we pay exclusive attention to what does not merit such attention, while we are unscrupulous in things which ought to concern us.

Our pride may be centered on our wealth and prosperity, our station in life, our fine clothes, our wit, beauty or strength. It may even grow out of our piety and good morals, as indicated by some of the above groupings.

Pride can ruin all the virtues and draw us into all kinds of disorders. The proud person is capable of any sin. "Pride goeth before destruction; and the spirit is lifted up before a fall." (*Prov.* 16:18). Therefore it is most necessary in the spiritual life to fight this vice in whatever guise it presents itself. If we permit it to enter our heart, the germs of all the vices enter with it, and we soon find ourselves a slave of Satan. We must beware of being ensnared by it, for the end of the proud, unrepentant sinner, as revealed by God, is the everlasting fire of Hell, in company with the demons.

Remedies for Pride

The only way to get the better of pride is to practice **humility**. It may sound like a contradiction, but the **humble man realizes that he is proud**, and earnestly strives to overcome the manifestations of pride in his life.

In striving for humility, we must always have before our eyes the example of Our Lord. We must keep in mind His promises in favor of the humble and the vengeance He reserves for the proud. We must cling to God and do His Will with all our soul. We must have recourse to prayer, again and again asking for this virtue. We must live in the presence of God, practice self-denial and the other Christian virtues, especially patience, forbearance, charity, meekness, submission, abandonment to God and conformity to His Will, sympathy, confidence in God, compunction for sin, modesty. We must not seek honors, but admit our nothingness and lack of virtue. We must be willing to accept humiliations and strive to seek God in all things.

Chapter 2

Covetousness or Avarice

COVETOUSNESS, or Avarice, is an inordinate love of worldly goods. It is a desire to accumulate and possess material things. It induces us to employ all sorts of means, just or unjust, in order to acquire them. Actually, it is a sign of mistrust in God and His Divine Providence.

If we are covetous, we do not love God, our neighbor, nor ourselves. We love **money** and **possessions**. We do not love and serve **God**, because no man can, at one and the same time, love and serve two masters: God and Mammon. We know this from the words of Christ. (*Matt.* 6:24). Neither do we love our **neighbor**, because we are ready to carry out, and we do carry out, any kind of injustice to increase our own fortune. We do not even love **our own self**, at least not our soul, for we do not use our possessions to add to our spiritual treasure, but to sell our soul

15

to the devil. If we do not love God, our neighbor, or ourself, we have no charity, and without charity how can we enter Heaven? Without charity, how can we fulfill our obligations to God? We will deny and forsake Him. Holy Scripture warns us, "The *desire* of money is the root of all evils." (*1 Tim.* 6:10).

Our inordinate love or covetousness may not be just for money, but for other things as well: books, pictures, china, cutlery, jewelry, cars, houses, real estate—anything. So whether we are rich or poor, we may be guilty of avarice or covetousness. And, as in the case of the others, this vice increases the more we gratify it.

We may discover this vice of avarice in ourselves by our hardness of heart toward the poor, or to our relatives, or in our reluctance to contribute to the support of the Church. We may discern it by our stingy use of what we have, or in our being too saving with what we ought to use. It may be found in our indifference to charitable works, in our want of zeal for what may cost us something, in our hoarding up money or whatever it is to which we are attached; in paying our debts grudgingly; in being dis-

turbed at trifling losses; in refusing to give
or lend.

The malice of the true miser is an obvi-
ous and revolting evil. He loses no opportunity to increase his wealth. He employs
every means to add to his savings, without
regard to justice or injustice. He lives a poor
and miserable life. He groans over the least
misfortune or loss. He has but one
thought—**his money**. And more often than
not, he dies in squalor and poverty, though
possessing a handsome fortune.

Probably we could not classify ourselves
as **misers**, but even lesser degrees of this
vice work havoc in our spiritual life. It blinds
us to the value of spiritual things. We have
no time nor taste for God when we are
always seeking material and temporal things.
Our Lord warns us in a parable that if we
are not watchful, the cares and riches of
this world will crowd out of our soul the
seeds of faith and piety. Our attachments
to possessions may result only in venial sins,
but real avarice is classified by St. Paul with
the **greatest** sins when he writes of those
who are "filled with all iniquity, malice,
fornication, *avarice,* wickedness, full of
envy, murder, contention, deceit, malignity,

whisperers, detractors, hateful to God, contumelious, proud, haughty, inventors of evil things, disobedient to parents, foolish, dissolute, without affection, without fidelity, without mercy." (*Rom.* 1:29-31).

The desire to possess is deeply rooted in our human nature. It is an appetite both hard to control and difficult to suppress. Under its impulse we find excuses everywhere to acquire possessions: our family must be provided for; we must look out for our old age; for our health; for our safety, our honor. We must have *some* pleasure! We may be led by avarice to resort to all kinds of means, lawful or unlawful, to acquire and guarantee the possession of the money, the property, the position we desire. We may lie, cheat, steal, take bribes, give false testimony, betray friends. We may resort to extortion, violence and murder. We may be cruel and hardhearted to the poor because we are intent only on getting more of what we covet, or at least on preserving what we have.

St. Thomas Aquinas points out that one person cannot have a super-abundance of the world's goods without another lacking what is necessary. We see proofs of this everywhere. When many people have a superabundance of earthly goods, there is injustice to others. Avarice causes much discontent and friction. It foments disunion between the rich and the poor.

Remedies for Avarice

We fight avarice with generosity, liberality, kindness, mercy. "Blessed are the merciful for they shall obtain mercy." (*Matt.* 5:7). Generosity bespeaks a healthy disposition of heart. It opens the door to greater love of God, to peace of mind, to consideration for others. Holy Scripture tells us, "It is a more blessed thing to give, rather than to receive." (*Acts* 20:35).

Even if we are not wealthy, we can wean our hearts from material things and spend less money on ourselves in order to be able to give something to the poor, to the missions, and to other works of charity. We need to practice charity and detachment in order not to become too much attached to things of this world. We must not let the anxieties of this life, with its riches, its vanity of honors and its passing pleasures, prevent or distract us from seeking the true riches of the life to come.

In conclusion, it may be well to add that covetousness may have a spiritual counterpart in our exercises of piety, when we seek only spiritual delight in them for ourselves. We ought rather to perform them with a desire to express our love for God and to fulfill His Will, which we know from the first lesson of the Catechism to be the purpose of our life on earth.

Chapter 3

Lust

LUST is generally spoken of as **impurity**. Impurity is a shameful vice because it changes a good and beautiful power into sin. This vice is opposed to chastity, which Our Lord tells us makes men like angels. Chastity is defined by St. Thomas as the virtue which regulates sensual desires and pleasures for the married and absolutely forbids them to the unmarried. Hence, lust or impurity is a seeking for unlawful pleasures, especially through the sense of touch. Sins of impurity defile both the soul and the body, which is the temple of the Holy Spirit, and is destined at the resurrection of the body to be glorified forever.

The modest ear is offended by the very names of sins committed through lust, such as adultery, fornication, incest, rape, birth control, abortion, solitary sin. St. Paul says of these, "Let it not so much as be named among you." (*Eph.* 5:3). We name them only to inspire horror for them.

Impurity wraps itself around all our senses and through them enters our soul. It blinds us to spiritual values, darkens our minds, weakens our wills and leads us to place a created good before God. We may commit sins of the **mind** by impure thoughts; sins of the **eyes** by giving in to curiosity, by impure looks at persons, pictures or things, by sinful reading; sins of the **ears** by listening to indecent speech, lewd and suggestive stories, jokes, songs, etc.; sins of the **nose*** by enjoyment of sensuous odors; sins of the **mouth** by impure words and songs and failure to chide evil talk; sins of the **lips** by sensuous kissing; sins of the **hands** by sinful touches, fondling, embraces, or other sinful actions; sins of the **heart** by impure desires and failure to repress impure sensations when unintentionally aroused; sins which we occasion in **others**; sins arising from **companions**.

Indulgence in impurity in any way is simply contrary to God's plan. Married persons,

---

*With regard to this list of sins of the mind, eyes, nose, etc., it must be borne in mind that consent of the will is necessary for the committing of sin; without consent there is no sin. —*Publisher*, 2000.

though lawfully enjoying the pleasures of
sex which are sanctified by the marital
union, must also observe chastity according
to their state by a reasonable self-control.
Any misconduct with regard to others is dou-
bly grievous for the married. Whether
chastity is the consecrated chastity of the
priesthood or the cloister, the chastity of the
unmarried, or the chastity of wedlock, we
must see it as a dedication of our powers
to the service of God. Then it will be an
influence for uplifting the world about us.

Impurity is often followed by other evils.
It blinds the mind, perverts the will and
hardens the heart. It causes inconstancy in
repentance, brings about aversion to God
because His law forbids the desired pleasure, and fosters an excessive love of the
things of this world. It causes mental anxiety through fear of future punishment. It
often leads to diseases and insanity. Disobedience, scandal and loss of faith may follow in its wake. Insincere Confessions and
sacrilegious Communions are often the
result of impure practices. Lust or impurity
probably causes the loss of more souls than
any other sin.

Vulgarity, sensuality and impurity are nurtured by idleness, by attachment to ease and comfort, by excess in eating and drinking. Obscene and suggestive literature, scandalous movies and T.V. programs, immodest pictures, sinful dancing, immodest clothing and companions may lead us into sinful actions. Too frequent association with the opposite sex, as in the case of persons "going steady" without expectation of early marriage, often occasions mortal sins of impurity.

Safeguards for Purity

It is one of the penalties of Original Sin that the struggle against impurity continues throughout life and demands a constant custody of the senses, of the thoughts, desires and speech. Modesty in dress, reserve in actions, and careful choice of entertainment are necessary safeguards for preserving purity in ourselves and others. The spirit of penance and self-denial, frequent recourse to the Sacraments, docility to the Holy Spirit and prayer, are all most necessary means to be employed as weapons in this battle. We cannot play with fire and not be burned; we cannot expose ourselves to impurity and not sin. With humility and self-distrust we must "fly" from the occasions of sin, for as Holy Scripture tells us, "He that loveth danger shall perish in it." (*Ecclus.* 3:27).

Bad thoughts, however filthy and abominable, are not sins. It is only by consenting to them that we commit sin. We shall never be overcome so long as we call on the holy Names of Jesus and Mary. During the assaults of temptation, it is most useful to renew our resolution of suffering death rather than offend God; it is also a good practice to sign ourselves repeatedly with the Sign of the Cross, and with holy water. It is of great help, too, to reveal the temptation to our confessor. But prayer is the best remedy of all, accompanied by cries for help to Jesus and Mary.

Chapter 4

Anger

ANGER is one of the passions of the **soul**. It proceeds from a real or imaginary offense which makes us want to "get even" with the offender. When the **desire for revenge** is not suppressed, it is a sin and a vice. It is opposed to charity and justice. Every kind of anger, however, is not a vice. An occasional fit of temper is not the **vice** of anger, but it may be a sin. There is also a form of anger that is good and virtuous, when it proceeds from a proper cause, as in the case of Our Lord driving the buyers and sellers from the Temple.

We have given way to anger and hate when we harbor resentment in our heart against a certain person or persons; when we plot harm for anyone by word or deed; when we use insulting language toward the offender. We are guilty of anger when we become excited and incensed to such a degree that we strike or hurt another; when we wrangle and quarrel violently with another; or when by the sullen expression on our face or by our silence, we show our resentment toward him. Our sin is very, very serious if we harbor rancor or hatred in our heart for days, or months, or even years and abstain from marks of kindness and friendship. We are also guilty of anger if we abuse our authority and punish an inferior more than he deserves. We may even direct our anger toward God interiorly, or exteriorly in passionate blasphemy.

Anger is a destructive and highly injurious vice. A fit of rage deprives us of reason; it estranges us from God. It separates us from friends and relatives. Anger clouds the intellect, and its unreasoning obstinacy makes us trample on the rights of others.

Anger destroys peace and produces disastrous wars. It causes all sorts of evils, discords, enmities, long-standing quarrels, insults, spites, slander, blasphemy, hatred, revenge, murder. All these things kill charity and are obstacles to grace, our greatest gift from God.

To Counteract Anger

If anger is our problem, we must find out why we are easily and often angered, and we must fight, watch and pray to overcome it. Whatever the offense may be, and whoever the offender, we must convince ourselves that God has permitted it in order to try us and to accustom us to practice meekness, thereby to increase our merits. Instead of giving in to the movements of rising anger, we must control ourselves and preserve self-possession, in order not to show signs of disturbance or betray animosity by word or action.

A spiritual writer gives this excellent advice: "Always have within yourself a peaceful retreat where you may extinguish every movement of anger. Thus, after an injury you must not only keep your lips silent, but you must observe an **inner** silence, and after having calmed yourself, strive to calm the agitation of the one who is angered against you. The memory of injury received must not be constantly renewed." (Dom Van Houtryve, O.S.B., in *Benedictine Peace*.)

To bring anger into check is to take a step toward bringing ourselves into subjection to God. An even temper attracts others and is a guarantee of quiet joy. "A soft answer turneth away wrath." If we are gentle and meek under provocation, we will appease the anger of the other person, who very likely may be upset too. We must always remember: God forbids all vengeance. If another has aroused our anger, we must forgive him from our heart. Our Lord teaches that we should look for an opportunity to show him a kindness, because doing good to others makes us love them, and such an action puts an exterior seal on our inward forgiveness.

We need the grace of God to overcome anger and to practice self-possession at all times. We must often beg God to grant us calmness, tranquility and peace, and call upon Him to help us quickly in moments of temptation.

If we are naturally quick-tempered, we must pay particular attention to the petition in the **Our Father** wherein we ask: "Forgive us our trespasses, **as we forgive** those who trespass against us," and make efforts to forgive others **from our heart**. This is the supernatural virtue of patient forbearance, meekness and forgiveness.

Anger is the daughter of offended pride that cannot bear contradiction, and of selfishness that seeks its own comfort and convenience. It is opposed to peace of mind, which is one of the requisites for progress in the spiritual life. Whether it takes the form of explosive irritation or sullen resentment, it has no place in the Christian life. Checking the slighter forms of impatience and irritability will go far in helping to forestall an outbreak of the passion of anger.

Chapter 5

Envy

ENVY is the root from which spring hatred, calumny, detraction, joy in another's misfortune, and distress at his prosperity. Every form of hate, strife, contention, quarreling, persecution, backbiting, jealousy, contempt, uncharitableness, malice and ill-will may proceed from it. Because they seem to lessen our own merits and right to esteem, we direct our envy against another's temporal goods and possessions, or against his spiritual gifts and good qualities.

This vice is greatly displeasing to God and most opposed to His grace, although we take too little heed of it. Essentially, it is ingratitude to God.

Envy proceeds from pride. We desire to be superior to the one we envy, so we are grieved over any good qualities he has and belittle them; we rejoice when some misfortune befalls him. We put an evil construction on what he says and does and expose any defects we observe in him.

Envy destroys charity in our heart, keeps us from advancing in perfection and renders us hateful to God. It makes us ungrateful, so that we do not give thanks for benefits shown us, but may even depreciate them.

Remedies for Envy

There is nothing more difficult to cure than envy, nothing that causes the soul more suffering, vexation and torment of mind. It gnaws at the heart like a worm. The chief remedies against it are fervent **prayer**, the practice of **humility** and reflection on the grievousness of this sin, the difficulty of its cure and the evils that flow from it. The lives of Saints will offer many inspirations.

The virtue opposed to envy is **charity** or **brotherly love**. Brotherly love causes us to consider our neighbor's interests as our own. It makes us willing to act and suffer for others, inspires a hearty sympathy in another's trials and sorrows and a willingness to assist him. It fills us with sincere joy in his successes and represses any feelings of rancor or ill-will that arise.

Envy is a tool of the devil, who goes about the world seeking the ruin of souls because he envies their good and wants to revenge himself against God by destroying them. If we do not want to be his tool, we must strive to make peace and love the fundamental rule of our relationship with others. We are all brothers before God, and by Baptism we have become members of the one Mystical Body of Christ. Hence, when we injure another, we sin against Our Lord and against our own self. We must see Christ in all men, if we are always to speak well of others, defend them and help them by acts of charity. We are all **one** Body, all seeking the same end—eternal life together in Heaven. And as we are all **one Body**, so we must all be animated by **one spirit,** the Spirit of Christ— the Holy Spirit, who is CHARITY.

Chapter 6

Gluttony

GLUTTONY is an unregulated love for food or drink. It is appetite out of order, by which we abuse the legitimate pleasure God has attached to eating and drinking. It is sometimes said that gluttony makes one "like an animal," though animals seldom overeat or drink too much. Yet there is some truth in this statement because gluttony dulls the **mind**, that is, the intellect and reason, which is the faculty that lifts us above animals.

Gluttony is the source of serious obstacles in our spiritual life. It is not easy to study or pray after eating or drinking too much. Gluttony weakens the will and fosters a spirit of laziness, sensuality and impurity. It often results in silliness and vulgar or obscene talk.

We may be what is called a "gourmand" by eating too much or consuming food too quickly and too avidly. We may be a "gourmet" by being too fastidious and wanting unusual foods and delicacies. We may commit small faults by being too finicky, difficult to please, critical or inclined to grumble about food.

Intoxication, or the excessive use of alcoholic drinks, which results in drunkenness, is the worst form of this vice. The drunkard drowns his reason in liquor so he no longer knows what he is doing. His evil habit causes him to lose his good name and makes others despise him. Very often it brings impoverishment, disgrace and starvation to the family. Anger, cursing, quarreling, fighting, stealing and cheating are often the result of the habit of drinking.

A man may beat his wife and children or others, or even commit murder because of this vice. Sins of impurity are closely allied to it. Countless auto accidents result from drunken driving. All too often these accidents bring injury and death to several persons. The drunkard not infrequently dies in a stupor, so he is not able to repent of his sins, and what then must be his eternal destiny? Holy Scripture says, "Do not err: neither fornicators, nor idolaters, nor adulterers, nor the effeminate, nor liers with mankind, nor thieves, nor covetous, nor *drunkards,* nor railers, nor extortioners shall possess the kingdom of God." (*1 Cor.* 6:9-10).

Unfortunately, drunkenness is not confined to the male sex, as it was notably in former years, but has become a common vice also among women, in whom it seems all the more degrading.

There are grades or degrees of intoxication. Complete drunkenness, which takes away the reason, is mortally sinful. Incomplete intoxication, when there is no grave disorder, may be less grievous. The degree of the **sin** is in accord with the degree of the **disorder**.

We may become party to the sin of another by inducing him to drink to excess, so we should take the greatest care in offering a drink as a mark of friendship and hospitality, or in serving liquor at social affairs. Above all, it is wrong to insist if a person refuses, or to offer strong drinks to the young.

Alcoholism with its many vicious consequences is one of the most widespread evils of our time. Men, women and youths are its victims. It ruins many homes by discord and divorce. It ruins the lives of all who are in its power.

The Church teaches that moderation and sobriety are always to be observed in the use of alcoholic beverages. For many, total abstinence is the only guarantee that they will not some day cross the line and become an alcoholic or a drunkard as a result of their first occasional and lawful indulgence.

In connection with this subject, abuse of drugs and narcotics may also be mentioned. Drugs and narcotics have a necessary use in illnesses, but should be taken only under a doctor's prescription because of the danger of forming a habit by their use.

Safeguarded by Moderation

In striving for temperance in eating and drinking, we have Our Lord's example of penance, sobriety, abstinence and mortification to inspire us; likewise the example of the Saints, who often practiced heroic abstinence, by which they brought their appetites into subjection, preserved liberty of soul and built up spiritual strength, vigor and courage.

Fasting or mortification and self-denial in the matter of food is commanded at certain times by the Church. Moderate or regulated fasting has a beneficial effect even on the health and strength of the body. It makes the mind alert and helps to restrain the lower passions. The practice of the other virtues is made easier, and it keeps us from habitual immortification to which we incline.

The pleasure in eating and drinking is not an end in itself, but a means to preserve life. The guiding principle in avoiding gluttony is the ancient rule of "eating to live"—not "living to eat." St. Paul exhorts us, "Whether you eat or drink, or whatsoever else you do, do all to the glory of God." (*1 Cor.* 10:31).

Chapter 7

Sloth

SLOTH is spiritual laziness, although it includes laziness of the body too. It is caused by a certain lack of trust in God and makes us indifferent in the use of the means necessary for our sanctification. It is an aversion to spiritual effort, which leads to the neglect of grace. Its worst effect is to make us put off our return to God after mortal sin. How many souls who have neglected their Easter duty, or have fallen away from the Church, go on, year after year, endangering their salvation because they cannot break the bonds of sloth!

Sloth resides in our mind and **will** and is the most dangerous of all vices because it makes us **refuse to co-operate with grace**. Sloth inclines us to habits of sin and leads us to despair of breaking away from their slavery. It may thus lead us to final impenitence and the loss of our soul.

Countless venial sins result from our luke-warmness, tepidity and indifference in God's service. These in turn further weaken our will, and we find ourselves caught in a net which we have no will to break.

We can recognize how sloth affects us by our faint-heartedness in spiritual matters; by our sluggish will; by our procrastination or putting things off until another time; by our dissipation and useless work, which is a sort of feverish activity that distracts us and does not allow time to attend to the needs of our soul; by our seeking bodily ease and comfort; by our idleness, or doing no good at all.

Sloth leads us to neglect the duties of our state. It makes us give up trying to carry out our resolutions. It makes us low-spirited and sad, because we know we are not using our graces. It makes us do things with a grumbling, grudging spirit because we are not generous in giving ourselves. It inclines us to much talking, because we do not want to call ourselves to account, and so we dissipate our spiritual forces and put off our "conversion."

The parable of the slothful servant, told by Our Lord in the Gospel of St. Matthew

(25:14-30), warns us of the dangers and sterility of sloth, and its end: **Hell.**

There are three chief forms of sloth: **occupation with unnecessary things**, which has been sufficiently touched upon above in explaining how we divert ourselves in this way so we have no time to listen to the voice of conscience; **distraction**; and **spiritual melancholy**.

Distraction destroys our recollection in prayer, leads us to fulfill our spiritual exercises without zeal and attention, and fills us with an overpowering weariness so that we postpone what we should do here and now. We see only an intolerable burden in our duties—not the privilege of doing them for God and storing up eternal merit in Heaven.

Spiritual melancholy, or depression, is a secret anger with ourselves and a species of self-love. Because of it, we have no courage to break with our faults and imperfections, with our habits of sin, and we feel a sense of despair. This in turn makes us quarrelsome and contentious. To get away from our inner conflict and anxiety, we turn to creatures and become preoccupied with unnecessary things, while we continue in our state of lukewarmness, procrastination and mediocrity or sin.

Our spiritual melancholy gives the devil power over our soul and is a condition of soul that easily leads to many grievous sins. It weakens and hinders the effects of the Sacraments. It makes the salutary means of the spiritual life act like poison. We cannot find God, and our unhappiness increases, though we are not really so much concerned with finding God as with finding His consolations. His will and His honor do not matter to us so much as our desires and our reputation. Our goal is not God, but our own spiritual peace or progress; that is, a spiritualized "self-seeking." We have lost sight of our true end and the way to it.

Father Faber says of this condition of soul: "Sadness is a sort of spiritual disability. A melancholy man can never be more than a convalescent in the House of God. God has rather to wait upon him as his Infirmarian than he to wait on God as His Father and King . . . There is no moral imbecility so great as that of querulousness and sentimentality. He who lies down at full length on life as if it were a sickbed—poor, languishing soul, what will he ever do for God?"

Today, sloth often goes by the name of

"escapism." The person who is the victim of sloth realizes he is in a spiritual fog and may try to blame it on spiritual dryness or some other cause, when it is an **inaction of the will which destroys love**.

We may flounder through a lifetime and never recognize that what is keeping us from spiritual advancement is sloth. No one will know how many are kept away from the Sacraments, or from daily Mass and Holy Communion, by sloth. No one can judge how much the spiritual and corporal works of mercy, upon which we are to be judged, are neglected because of sloth, but it is certain that this vice works havoc in countless ways.

Even the sloth of mind which makes us neglect to occupy our intellect with useful things or serious work is very dangerous, because a mind that is not so occupied tends to evil, and nothing stops its rapid descent. Our mind may be occupied with culpable thoughts even when our body is busy. On the other hand, sloth of body, or idleness and inactivity, may lead to a thousand temptations which we will be unable to resist because of the weakness and sluggishness of our will, sleeping in the inaction of sloth.

We must fly sloth because it prevents us from working out our salvation; because it is the parent of many evils. If we sow nothing, we shall reap nothing. Life is short, and the years are few for meriting the eternal joys of Heaven. We must follow the example of Our Lord who won the glory of Heaven by toils and penances, by His Passion and Cross. To fail to store up eternal merits is to lessen our merit in Heaven; to fail to do penance for our sins is to prepare ourselves for a long Purgatory; and to fail in attaining our eternal salvation is to fail utterly and reap the eternal woe of damnation.

Diligence or zeal in working for God and the good of souls is the virtue contrary to sloth. It brings ease and joy in fulfilling our religious duties. The light of faith is nourished with the oil of good works. It enables us to avoid many temptations and sins and helps ensure our final perseverance.

Remedy for Sloth

In combating sloth, we must use violence against our inclinations to laziness, and seek help in prayer and the Sacraments. We must remember the Day of Judgment. Spiritual reading will help to stir up our sluggish will; but above all, devotion to the Holy Spirit will be effective, because fear, not love, motivates sloth, and the Holy Spirit is the Spirit of Love, the Source to whom we must go to find the antidote to sloth, namely, Divine Love. We must beg Him to pour forth love into our hearts.

Chapter 8

The Seven Roots of Sin

ALL our sins are traceable to these seven roots, the Seven Capital Sins. These seven sources of sin have been compared to diseases that affect the body. **Pride** is a spiritual **cancer** that eats and consumes the vital life. **Covetousness** is like spiritual **consumption** or tuberculosis, wasting away the soul's inner powers. **Lust** is a spiritual **leprosy**. **Anger** is a delirious **fever**. **Envy** is spiritual **blood-poisoning**. **Gluttony** leads to a **sleeping-sickness** that may end in death. **Sloth** is like a **paralysis** of the soul that hinders its progress and causes neglect of the means of grace, indifference, and even final impenitence. It is pride and sloth that are the parents of final impenitence.

True understanding of the nature and effects of the Capital Sins is the first step in combating them. Let us take up arms now and go to the battle! We will be what we **will** to be!

Chapter 9

Jesus, Our Model

PICTURE to yourself in your heart His behavior and His actions: How meek and quiet in His manner among all classes of men; how genial among His own; how reserved in His eating and drinking; how full of feeling for the poor, to whom He was in all things like, who belonged to His own inner circle. How He turned no one aside; how He shrank from none, not even the leper, not even the sinner, not even the shameful, not even the shameless!

How He paid no court to the great; how He was obsequious to none! How He kept Himself aloof from the cares of the world! How He troubled Himself in nothing for the needs of the body! How restrained were His eyes; how patient He stood under insult; how gentle His answers! How He would not vindicate His honor by a sharp or bitter reply! How He turned away malice by calm and quiet, by assertion of truth, by the offer of His love! Again, how composed His every movement, how faultless in every action!

How He longed for the salvation of souls, for the love of whom He had willed to become man and had willed to die! How in all His behavior He was a model of all good, the light of all men, their WAY, their TRUTH, their LIFE!

Again, how He endured labor and want and hunger and thirst and utter weariness! How compassionate He was with all who suffered! How He adapted Himself to the weak, how He stooped to the lowly! How He avoided scandal. How He refused no sinner. How kindly He welcomed every penitent. How peaceful in all His words, how encouraging to good will; how stern to hard hearts. How earnest in prayer, how quick to do a service, saying of Himself, "I am in the midst of you as He that serveth."

Again, how long His hours of prayer. How obedient to His parents. How He shunned every sign of boasting, every show of being singular. How He avoided all this world's glory, all this world's power, all this world's means to success!

All this, and much more, comes to the

mind when we think of Him. In Him we find a model for our every word and deed, moving or standing, seated, eating, silent or speaking, alone or with others. Study Him and you will grow in His love. In His company you will gain sweetness and confidence, and you will be strengthened in every virtue.

Let this be your wisdom, this your meditation, this your study: to have Him always in mind, to move you to imitation, to win you to His love.

—Archbishop Goodier, S.J.

Prayers

For the Seven Gifts of
the Holy Spirit

O LORD Jesus Christ, Who before ascending into Heaven didst promise to send the Holy Spirit to finish Thy work in the souls of Thine Apostles and disciples, deign to grant the same Holy Spirit to me, that He may perfect in my soul the work of Thy grace and Thy love.

Grant me the Gift of **Wisdom**, that I may despise the perishable things of this world and aspire only after the things that are eternal; the Gift of **Understanding**, to enlighten my mind with the light of Thy Divine truth; the Gift of **Counsel**, that I may ever choose the surest ways of pleasing God and gaining Heaven; the Gift of **Fortitude**, that I may bear my cross with Thee and may overcome with courage all the obstacles that oppose my salvation; the Gift of **Knowledge**, that I may know God and know myself, and grow perfect in the science of the Saints; the Gift

51

of **Piety**, that I may find the service of God sweet and amiable; the Spirit of **Fear**, that I may be filled with a loving reverence toward God, and may dread in any way to displease Him.

Mark me, dear Lord, with the sign of Thy true disciples, and animate me in all things with Thy Spirit. Amen.

To the Blessed Virgin Mary
For Acquiring Virtues

O MARY, Mother of Mercy, others may ask of thee what they please—bodily health, worldly goods and advantages—but I ask for whatever thou seest to be most needful for me and what is most in conformity with thy pure heart. Thou art so humble; obtain for me humility and love of contempt. Thou wert so patient under the sufferings and trials of life; obtain for me patience and fortitude. Thou wert most charitable toward your neighbor; obtain for me charity toward all, and particularly toward those who are in any way my enemies. Thou art filled with the love of God; obtain for me the gift of His pure and holy love.

Thou art entirely united to the Divine

Will; obtain for me complete conformity to the Will of God in all things. Thou art the holiest of all creatures, O Mary; make me a saint.

Love for me is not wanting on thy part; thou canst do all and thou hast the will to obtain all for me. The only thing, then, that can prevent me from receiving thy favors is neglect on my part in having recourse to thee, or too little confidence in thine intercession. These gifts I ask of thee, hoping with the greatest confidence to receive them, O Mary, my Mother, my hope, my love, my life, my refuge, my help and my consolation. Amen.

Prayers for Humility

To God the Father

O GOD, Who dost resist the proud and give Thy grace to the humble, endow me with that true virtue of humility of which Thy Divine Son gave us a living example. Let me never provoke Thee to anger by my pride, but make me always conscious of my lowliness and unworthiness and of my total dependence on Thee. Amen.

To Our Lord

O MY most humble Jesus, Who for love of me didst humble Thyself and become obedient unto the death of the Cross, how dare I appear before Thee and call myself Thy follower when I see myself so proud that I cannot bear a single slight without resenting it! How, indeed, can I be proud, when by my sins I have so often deserved to be cast into the abyss of Hell! O Jesus, meek and humble of heart, help me and make me like unto Thee.

Thou, for love of me, didst bear so many insults and injuries. I, for love of Thee, will bear slights and humiliations patiently. But Thou dost see, O Jesus, how proud I am in my thoughts, how disdainful in my words, how ambitious in my deeds. Grant me true humility of heart and a clear knowledge of my own nothingness. May I, for love of Thee, rejoice at being despised and feel no resentment when others are preferred before me. Let me not be filled with pride when I am praised, but seek only to be great in Thy sight and to please Thee in all things. Amen.

To Obtain Detachment from Earthly Goods

O JESUS, who didst choose a life of poverty and obscurity, grant me the grace to keep my heart detached from the transitory things of this world. Be Thou henceforth my only treasure, for Thou art infinitely more precious than all other possessions. My heart is too solicitous for the vain and fleeting things of earth. Make me always mindful of Thy warning words: "What does it profit a man if he gain the whole world, but suffer the loss of his own soul?" Grant me the grace to keep Thy holy example always before my eyes, that I may despise the nothingness of this world and make Thee the object of all my desires and affections. Amen.

Prayers for Purity

To St. Joseph

GUARDIAN of virgins and holy father St. Joseph, to whose faithful custody Christ Jesus, innocence itself, and Mary, Virgin of virgins, were committed, I pray and beseech thee, by these dear pledges, Jesus and Mary, that being preserved from all impurity, I may with spotless mind, pure heart and chaste body, ever most chastely serve Jesus and Mary all the days of my life. Amen.

To St. Aloysius

SAINT Aloysius, adorned with angelic virtues, I commend to thee most earnestly the chastity of my mind and body. I pray thee, by thine angelic purity, to commend me to the Immaculate Lamb, Jesus Christ, and to His most holy Mother, the Virgin of virgins, and to protect me from every grievous sin. Permit me not to defile myself by any spot of impurity; and when thou seest me in temptation or in danger of sin, banish far from my heart every unclean thought and desire. Awaken in me the thought of eternity and of Jesus Crucified; imprint deeply in my heart a lively sense of the holy fear of God; set me on fire with the love of God and grant me the grace to imitate thee on earth, that I may enjoy the possession of God with thee in Heaven. Amen.

Prayer to Overcome Sloth and Lukewarmness

O MY GOD, I know well that so negligent a life as mine cannot please Thee. I know that by my lukewarmness I have closed the door to the graces which Thou dost desire to bestow upon me. O my God, do not reject me, as I deserve, but continue to be merciful toward me, and I will make great efforts to amend and to arise from this miserable state. In the future I will be more careful to overcome my passions and to follow Thine inspirations; and never through slothfulness will I omit my duties, but will strive to fulfill them with greater diligence and fidelity. In short, I will from this time forward do all I can to please Thee, and will neglect nothing which I know to be pleasing to Thee.

Since Thou, O my Jesus, hast been so liberal with Thy graces toward me and hast deigned to give Thy Blood and Thy Life for me, I am sorry for having acted with so little generosity toward Thee, Who art worthy of all honor and all love. But, O my Jesus, Thou knowest my weakness. Help me with Thy powerful grace; in Thee I confide.

O Immaculate Virgin Mary, help me to overcome myself and to become a saint. Amen.

Prayer of a Soul Enslaved by Bad Habits

BEHOLD me, O my God, at Thy feet! I do not deserve mercy, but, O my Redeemer, the Blood which Thou hast shed for me encourages and obliges me to hope for it. How often I have offended Thee, and yet I have again fallen into the same sin.

O my God, I wish to amend, and in order to be faithful to Thee, I will place all my confidence in Thee. I will, whenever I am tempted, instantly have recourse to Thee. Hitherto, I have trusted in my own promises and resolutions and have neglected to recommend myself to Thee in my temptations. This has been the cause of my repeated failures. From this day forward, be Thou, O Lord, my strength, and thus I shall be able to do all things, for "I can do all things in Him who strengthens me."

To Overcome Some Vice
Such as Intemperance or Impurity

O GOD, who didst break the chains of blessed Peter the Apostle, and didst make him come forth unscathed, loose the bonds of Thy servant, (*Name*), held in captivity by the vice of (*name it*); and by the merits of the same Apostle, do Thou grant me (*him, her*) to be delivered from its tyranny. Remove from my (*his, her*) heart all excessive love for sensual pleasures and gratifications, so that living soberly, justly and piously, I (*he, she*) may attain to everlasting life with Thee. Amen.

Against Evil Thoughts

ALMIGHTY and all-merciful God, look favorably upon our prayers and free our hearts from temptation to evil thoughts, that we may deserve to be accounted worthy dwelling places of the Holy Spirit. Shed upon our hearts the brightness of Thy grace, that we may ever think thoughts worthy of Thy majesty and pleasing to Thee, and ever sincerely love Thee. Through Christ Our Lord. Amen.

For Remission of Sins

O GOD, Who dost reject no one, but art appeased in Thy tender mercy by the repentance of the greatest sinners, mercifully regard our humble prayers, and enlighten our hearts that we may be able to fulfill Thy Commandments. Through Christ Our Lord. Amen.

God Knows

JESUS, when it is very hard,
When the body is tired,
When the mind is clouded,
When the soul is troubled,
When I am a weary burden to myself,
When I am a scandal to others,
When my best friends seem to be against me,
When every door is closed:

Then let me remember myself,
What I am and what I deserve.
My nothingness, fit only to be trodden on,
My fickleness, utterly unreliable,
My sinfulness, meriting a worse doom,
My selfishness, always seeking its own,
My cruelty to others in like state,

And let me see Your hand in it all.

Let me remember You,
Who You are and what You deserve,
And yet what You have received.
Whom none could accuse of sin,
Yet Who found Yourself a scandal to many.
Who would not break a bruised reed,
Yet Whose soul was made sorrowful unto
   death.
Who for me despised the shame
And endured the Cross.

Let me remember my Father
Who is faithful,
Who will not try me more than I am able,
Who ruleth from end to end mightily
And disposeth all things sweetly.
Who out of evil will draw good,
Who is sweet and gentle
And of much mercy to all who will love Him.
         —Archbishop Goodier, S.J.

Prayer for Grace

O MY GOD, remember that moment when for the first time Thou didst pour Thy grace into my heart, washing me of Original Sin that Thou mightest receive me into the number of Thy children. O God, Thou Who art my Father, grant me in Thine infinite mercy, through the merits and the Blood of Jesus Christ, and through the sorrows of the holy Virgin Mary, the graces which Thou dost desire that I should receive this day for Thy greater glory and my salvation. Amen.

O HEART of Love, I place all my trust in Thee; for though I fear all things from my own weakness, I hope all things from Thy goodness.

O PUREST Heart of the Blessed Virgin Mary, obtain for me from Jesus a pure and humble heart.

If you have enjoyed this book, consider making your next selection from among the following . . .

Moments Divine—Before Blessed Sacrament. *Reuter* . . 8.50
Raised from the Dead—400 Resurrection Miracles. 16.50
Wonder of Guadalupe. *Johnston* 7.50
St. Gertrude the Great. 1.50
Mystical City of God. (abr.) *Agreda* 18.50
Abortion: Yes or No? *Grady, M.D.* 2.00
Who Is Padre Pio? *Radio Replies Press* 2.00
What Will Hell Be Like? *St. Alphonsus* 75
Life and Glories of St. Joseph. *Thompson* 15.00
Autobiography of St. Margaret Mary. 6.00
The Church Teaches. *Documents* 16.50
The Curé D'Ars. *Abbé Francis Trochu* 21.50
What Catholics Believe. *Lovasik* 5.00
Clean Love in Courtship. *Lovasik* 2.50
History of Antichrist. *Huchede.* 4.00
Self-Abandonment to Div. Prov. *de Caussade* 18.00
Canons & Decrees of the Council of Trent 15.00
Love, Peace and Joy. *St. Gertrude/Prévot* 7.00
St. Joseph Cafasso—Priest of Gallows. *St. J. Bosco* . . . 5.00
Mother of God and Her Glorious Feasts. *O'Laverty* . . . 10.00
Apologetics. *Glenn* 10.00
Isabella of Spain. *William Thomas Walsh* 20.00
Philip II. H.B. *William Thomas Walsh* 37.50
Fundamentals of Catholic Dogma. *Ott* 21.00
Holy Eucharist. *St. Alphonsus* 10.00
Hidden Treasure—Holy Mass. *St. Leonard* 5.00
St. Philomena. *Mohr* 8.00
St. Philip Neri. *Matthews* 5.50
Martyrs of the Coliseum. *O'Reilly* 18.50
Thirty Favorite Novenas 75
Devotion to Infant Jesus of Prague 75
On Freemasonry *(Humanum Genus). Leo XIII* 1.50
Thoughts of the Curé D'Ars. *St. John Vianney* 2.00
Way of the Cross. *St. Alphonsus Liguori.* 1.00
Way of the Cross. *Franciscan* 1.00
Magnificent Prayers. *St. Bridget of Sweden* 2.00
Conversation with Christ. *Rohrbach* 10.00
Douay-Rheims New Testament 15.00
Life of Christ. 4 vols. H.B. *Emmerich* 60.00
The Ways of Mental Prayer. *Lehodey* 14.00

At your Bookdealer or direct from the Publisher.
Call Toll-Free 1-800-437-5876.